Tools for Managing Change

First Edition

Kate Nelson and Stacy Aaron

Change Guides LLC

© 2005 by Change Guides LLC
Any reproduction of any part of this
publication without the written consent
of Change Guides LLC is prohibited
ISBN 0-9767359-0-3
Cover Design, Layout, and
Graphics by Jody Johnson

Printed in the USA 2011
Change Guides LLC
www.changeguidesllc.com
E-mail: guides@changeguidesllc.com
513-354-9503

Acknowledgments

We would like to thank our colleagues for all of the input and support we have received during the creation of this book. Many people have shared their insights, provided their support and contributed their services to our efforts.

We would also like to thank the countless clients and students we have worked with during our combined 30 years of experience. They have helped us refine our thinking about change management and the tools that help us get the work of change management done. This book is a more insightful and useful resource because of our collaborations.

Contents

The Importance of Change Management 5

Who Should Use the Change Management Pocket Guide 6

How the Change Management Pocket Guide is Organized 7

How to Use the Change Management Pocket Guide Tools 9

Plan Tools:

Change Readiness Audit 12

Stakeholder Analysis 18

Commitment Assessment 23

Leadership Alignment Assessment 27

Strengths, Weaknesses, Opportunities,
Threats (SWOT) Analysis.......................................32

Change Management Workplan 38

HR Infrastructure Checklist....................................42

Communication Plan 46

Key Message Worksheet 53

Leadership Involvement Plan 59

Do Tools:

One-Minute Exchange Form 66

Communication Network Table 70

Road Show Agenda..75

Feedback Form 78

Frequently Asked Questions (FAQ) Sheet.................82

3

Contents

Implementation Checklist 88

Stakeholder Commitment Meeting Template............92

Workforce Transition Plan 96

Training Needs Assessment 100

Sustain Tools:

Systems and Structure Action Plan......................108

Rewards and Measures Alignment Template 113

Roles and Responsibility Template 118

Knowledge Sharing Agreement............................123

Change Integration Checklist 132

HR Measures Form..136

HR Measures Questionnaire 141

Lessons Learned Process....................................146

About the Authors 149

INTRODUCTION

Change Management Pocket Guide Introduction

➤ *The Importance of Change Management*

Successful Change Management is the discipline of driving business results by changing behaviors. Whether you are launching new information technology, applying an innovative work process or completing a merger transaction, effective Change Management is essential to your success. Leaders and project teams must understand the human dynamics of change and prepare for the emotional response it can generate.

To achieve strong business results, you ultimately need people who are committed to success, motivated to get results, and who possess the knowledge and tools to get the job done. People naturally resist changes to their comfortable routine. New ideas and mindsets about how to work and an individual's role within the organization can create uncertainty and stress.

Your challenge is to apply effective Change Management principles to anticipate and manage resistance. By doing so, you can achieve the organization's ultimate goals to:

- Accelerate the pace of change to achieve timely business outcomes and financial returns,
- Address and mitigate risk,
- Improve decision making,

5

INTRODUCTION

- Minimize the short-term dip in employee productivity and increase long-term productivity, and
- Strengthen the dynamic and adaptive responses of the organization and build the organization's ability to handle change in the future.

➤ *Who Should Use the Change Management Pocket Guide*

This Pocket Guide is intended for project managers and project team members already working to implement changes in their business. It is not, however, a primer on Change Management.

We developed this Pocket Guide with certain assumptions about your organization and the project team using it:

- The organization has defined an overall strategic direction or vision,
- There is someone accountable for managing the change,
- The project goals are clear,
- The project has leadership visibility and sponsorship, and
- The team has set a project timeline and milestones.

➤ How the Change Management Pocket Guide is Organized

The Change Management Pocket Guide is organized using the Change Management 101 Model™. This model illustrates the three primary phases of Change Management project implementation: Plan, Do and Sustain. You must Plan the change process, Do the work required to lead the organization through transition, and Sustain new structures and behaviors to meet long-term business objectives.

The Change Management 101 Model™

Each phase includes two specific stages necessary to the change process. As you move from one stage to the next, you can use the tools in this Pocket Guide to gather information, set milestones and measure progress.

INTRODUCTION

THE PLAN PHASE

The two major stages of the Plan phase are to assess the needs of the organization and to develop plans to help change behaviors. Proper planning will help you identify the workforce issues related to the proposed change before they impede progress.

THE DO PHASE

The primary goals of the Do phase are to launch communication and transition the work. Effective communication and transition activities will create a receptive environment for change and facilitate smooth implementation.

THE SUSTAIN PHASE

The most often overlooked aspect of any change project is the Sustain phase, during which your team aligns structures and integrates new ways of working into the business. If the organization fails to sustain new behaviors, business benefits will likely not be realized or they will be short lived.

INTRODUCTION

➤ *How To Use The Change Management Pocket Guide Tools*

In each stage of our Change Management Model, we offer four or five tools to focus your effort. Again, you can adapt these tools to fit your needs. Every tool in this Pocket Guide includes the following information to help clarify its purpose and use:

- **Name** of the tool,
- **What** it is,
- **Why** the tool is important,
- **When** to use it,
- **How** to implement it,
- **Successful Outcomes** to gauge progress when using the tool,
- **Tips & Lessons Learned** to share insights from the field,
- **What's Next** to guide how outputs can facilitate change,
- **The Tool**

PLAN

Plan: Assess Needs

A plan that addresses the needs of individuals and the organization must be developed in order to change behaviors. A critical element to planning is assessing the needs of individuals and the organization. Tools used to assess Change Management needs include:

- Change Readiness Audit
- Stakeholder Analysis
- Commitment Assessment
- Leadership Alignment Assessment
- Strengths, Weaknesses, Opportunities, Threats (SWOT) Analysis

The Change Management 101 Model™

Assess Needs

PLAN

➤ *Change Readiness Audit*

WHAT

- The Change Readiness Audit is a survey that evaluates the level of organizational readiness for change.

WHY

- To shape the Change Management Workplan by helping the team determine what activities will most effectively manage the change

- To highlight issues and areas that need further investigation

- To help the project team focus on critical areas

- To take a snapshot of how effectively change is being implemented

WHEN

- Conduct the audit during the Assess Needs Stage.

- Update or reference the audit throughout the project.

☛ How

1. Determine whether a formal or informal Change Readiness Audit is required (A formal assessment is recommended when a thorough, data-driven and robust assessment is required. An informal assessment may be appropriate when time and resources are short and a more subjective assessment is adequate).

Assess Needs

PLAN

- *If the Change Readiness Audit is being used as a formal assessment:*

    2. Define the target audience that will be impacted by the change.

    3. Define the survey population (either a random sample of the target audiences or only specific elements or levels of target audiences).

    4. Define the approach for implementing the survey (written or electronic survey alone, or focus groups and survey combined).

    5. Administer survey.

    6. Prepare a summary of the assessment findings and present the results to project leaders and champions.

    7. Determine what areas need further investigation and use other assessments (i.e. Leadership Alignment Assessment, Commitment Assessment) as needed.

    8. Develop action plans to address any item or category that has several "no" or "somewhat" answers.

    9. Incorporate actions into the Change Management Workplan.

Assess Needs

PLAN

- *If the Change Readiness Audit is being used as an informal assessment:*

  2. On a regular basis or when issues arise, review the checklist and answer questions with individuals or small groups to determine areas of risk.

  3. Determine what areas need further investigation and use other assessments (i.e. Leadership Alignment Assessment, Commitment Assessment) as needed.

  4. Develop action plans to address any item or category that has several "no" or "somewhat" answers.

  5. Modify the Change Management Workplan if necessary to reflect action plans.

  6. Routinely assess organizational readiness for the change by scoring the checklist.

★ SUCCESSFUL OUTCOMES

- When checks on the assessment tool move from "no" or "somewhat" to "yes"

- When the team agrees on actions that develop areas not yet ready for change and that leverage areas already prepared for change

PLAN

🖉 TIPS & LESSONS LEARNED

- Leverage existing meetings to administer the Change Readiness Audit as an informal assessment.

- Color the "yes" column green, the "somewhat" column yellow, and the "no" column red to visually demonstrate areas of risk if desired.

- Laminate a survey form and use erasable markers to score the checklist as an informal assessment to allow for repeated use.

- Solicit feedback from team members and stakeholders.

- Set realistic expectations about how results will be used.

- Tailor the survey where appropriate to link questions to a specific change or project.

- If the Change Readiness Audit categories below score several answers of "no" or "somewhat", use the assessment tool that follows to gather more data about underlying issues:

  - Vision and Business Case: Leadership Alignment Assessment
  - Leadership: Leadership Alignment Assessment
  - Engagement: Stakeholder Analysis, Commitment Assessment
  - Implementation Effectiveness: SWOT Analysis
  - Sustainability: SWOT Analysis

WHAT'S NEXT

- The results of the Change Readiness Audit should help focus further assessment activities and feed Change Management planning.

Assess Needs

15

PLAN

✂ The Tool: Change Readiness Audit

	Yes	Somewhat	No
Vision and Business Case			
• Is there a complete and unambiguous vision /future state?			
• Are employees excited about the future?			
• Do people understand how the change will benefit customers and stakeholders?			
• Is there a clear expectation of what successful change looks like?			
• Is there a clear understanding of the need for change?			
• Are there consistent and supportive messages from management on the need for change?			
Engagement			
• Is there recognition of who needs to be committed to the change in order to be successful?			
• Is there adequate participation by middle and lower managers in designing the future state?			
• Are there allowances for ensuring that involvement will not cause undue stress on the organization?			
• Is there a safe outlet for feedback including reactions, concerns and comments?			
Leadership			
• Is there a leadership team that is accountable for the success of the change?			
• Do leaders demonstrate commitment to the change through actions as well as words?			

16   Assess Needs

PLAN

	Yes	Somewhat	No
• Are leaders willing to commit resources to the implementation and sustainability of the change?			
• Do leaders invest their personal time and attention to following through on actions related to the change?			
Implementation Effectiveness			
• Are there enough resources to carry out the strategies (people, time and money)?			
• Are there well trained people with time available within the company to carry out /apply the tools?			
• Is there a means of measuring successful change?			
Sustainability			
• Is there an understanding of how to sustain the change through modifying HR systems (such as staffing, training, appraisal, rewards, communication)?			
• Have new measurement and reward systems been implemented?			
• Have new training and development systems been implemented?			
• Is the organization structure appropriate for the future state?			
• Does the organization have the skills/competencies to get the job done?			
• Is there understanding of how to sustain the change among leaders?			
• Is there a plan for adapting the change over time to shifting circumstances?			

Assess Needs

PLAN

➤ *Stakeholder Analysis*

WHAT

• A Stakeholder Analysis is a template and process that defines the people who are critical to a successful change and assesses their current and desired levels of support.

WHY

• To identify current and required levels of support for change by key stakeholders and stakeholder groups

• To better understand and begin responding to the Engagement portion of the Change Readiness Audit

• To provide a starting point for the Communication Plan and to gain additional information for the Change Management Workplan

WHEN

• Conduct the analysis during the Assess Needs Stage.

• Update or reference the analysis throughout the project.

☛ How

1. Develop a comprehensive list of stakeholders and list them in the Stakeholder Analysis tool. To define stakeholders, answer the following questions:

   - Who will be impacted by the project?
   - Who will be the 'customer' of the change?
   - Who will be required to work differently?

Assess Needs

PLAN

  - Who will use the project outputs?
  - Who will provide inputs to the project?
  - Who has influence over the project's success or failure?
  - Who has formal authority over the groups impacted?
  - Who has informal authority over the groups impacted?

2. Identify and circle those stakeholders that are key. Consider those individuals or groups who control critical resources, who can block change directly or indirectly, who must approve certain aspects of the change strategy, who shape the thinking of other critical constituents, or who own a key work process impacted by the change initiative.

3. Indicate where each key stakeholder is currently with regard to the change initiative with a C (current location).

4. Discuss where each stakeholder must be for the change initiative to be successful and indicate that location with a D (desired location).

5. Define what is important to stakeholders who are far from their desired level of support for the project.

★ SUCCESSFUL OUTCOMES

- When key stakeholders can be defined as strongly supportive or at the internalization stage in your stakeholder analysis

- When the tool provides clarity to the project team about whom the key stakeholders are and their respective levels of commitment to the change

---

Assess Needs

19

PLAN

✐ TIPS & LESSONS LEARNED

- Revisit the stakeholder analysis and update it regularly to determine if key stakeholders are evolving.

- Broaden your idea of traditional stakeholders. They can be any individuals or organizations – either inside or outside your own organization – who are involved in or affected by the change or who influence its success.

- If you are uncertain of the current and desired levels of support for the project, use a Commitment Assessment to gather feedback directly from stakeholders.

- Focus on understanding how key individuals view the merits of the change or the level of their project exposure and information, not on grading people. Use discretion when deciding if and how to share this information with others, especially those outside of the team.

- Consider *when* different stakeholders need to commit to the change and decide whose support is needed most urgently.

- Weightings can enhance the tool if desired by ranking the level of importance of each stakeholder.

PLAN

- If the levels of commitment in this template are not easily understood within the organization, the following labels may also be used:

    - Strongly Against, Moderately Against, Neutral, Moderately Supportive, Strongly Supportive

    - Actively Resisting, Wants it to Fail, Does not Care, Wants it to Succeed, Actively Helping the Project

WHAT'S NEXT

- The results of the Stakeholder Analysis should feed communication planning, leadership involvement planning and Change Management planning.

Assess Needs

PLAN

✂ The Tool: Stakeholder Analysis

NAME	Role & Function	Issues Concerns	Contact	Awareness	Understanding	Desire	Adoption	Internalization

PLAN

➤ Commitment Assessment

WHAT

- The Commitment Assessment is a self-assessment that allows people to plot their level of commitment to the change on a continuum and provide feedback on what would help them develop stronger commitment.

WHY

- To help understand the level of commitment of stakeholders and to gather feedback on ways to help increase commitment to the change

- To better understand and begin responding to the Engagement portion of the Change Readiness Audit

- To help gather more detailed information for a Stakeholder Analysis

WHEN

- Conduct the assessment during the Assess Needs Stage.

- Ask people to update their self-assessment throughout the project.

☛ How

1. Refer to the Stakeholder Analysis and the Engagement portion of the Change Readiness Audit to determine which audiences require additional investigation into their levels of commitment to the change.

Assess Needs

23

PLAN

2. Determine the appropriate approach for administering the self-assessment. There are two options:

   - Prepare a large wall chart or poster of the assessment and have stakeholders apply post-it notes or colored dots to the poster

   - Give stakeholders individual copies of the assessment to complete

3. Ask audience members to evaluate their current level of commitment to the change using the Commitment Assessment Tool. Have them define two things they can do as individuals to increase their commitment to the change. Then ask them to define two things the team can do to increase their commitment.

4. Incorporate the findings of the Commitment Assessment into the Stakeholder Analysis where necessary.

5. Develop action plans to address issues or gaps identified and incorporate those actions into the Change Management Workplan.

★ SUCCESSFUL OUTCOMES

- When stakeholders consistently rate themselves as adopting or internalizing the change

- When the tool provides clarity to the team about stakeholders' levels of commitment and actions can be defined to help build commitment

- When the team agrees on actions to build commitment for stakeholders

PLAN

✎ TIPS & LESSONS LEARNED

- With a large group, asking people to mark responses on a wall chart may result in the group members following the first respondent's lead rather than reflecting on their true level of commitment.

- Not all stakeholders need to have the highest level of commitment on the continuum. Internalization is required for people who will need to change their behaviors; however, the business results might not require all stakeholders to change their behaviors (sometimes 70 or 80 percent is enough). Define the requirements for your project before focusing too much on small numbers of people who are not supportive.

- The following are simple definitions of the levels of commitment used in the assessment:

Stages of Commitment	
Contact:	• People have heard a change is in the works
Awareness:	• People are aware of the change's basic scope and concepts
Understanding:	• People understand the impact of the change to the organization and to their specific group
Desire:	• People understand the personal impact and "what's in it for me" and are willing to make that change happen
Adoption:	• People start to actually work in the new ways that are needed for the change to be successful
Internalization:	• People make the change their own and think of ways to build on the change to make it even better

WHAT'S NEXT

- The results of the Commitment Assessment should feed Change Management planning.

Assess Needs

25

PLAN

The Tool: Commitment Assessment

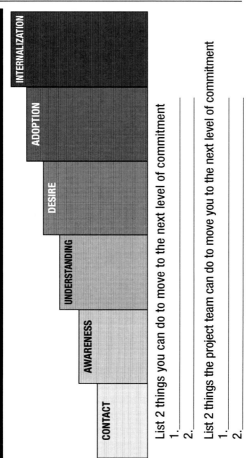

INTERNALIZATION

ADOPTION

DESIRE

UNDERSTANDING

AWARENESS

CONTACT

List 2 things you can do to move to the next level of commitment

1. _____
2. _____

List 2 things the project team can do to move you to the next level of commitment

1. _____
2. _____

Assess Needs

PLAN

➤ *Leadership Alignment Assessment*

WHAT

- The Leadership Alignment Assessment is an interview questionnaire that helps determine the degree of leadership agreement about the change.

WHY

- To determine the degree of leadership alignment around the change and identify gaps in the perception of leadership and staff about leadership alignment

- To better understand and begin responding to the Leadership portion of the Change Readiness Audit

WHEN

- Conduct the assessment during the Assess Needs Stage.

- Update or reference the assessment throughout the project.

☛ HOW

1. Determine the appropriate audience for the assessment based on the results of the Stakeholder Analysis and the Leadership portion of the Change Readiness Audit.

2. Based on information from the Leadership portion of the Change Readiness Audit, refine the survey questions to further investigate issues of concern.

3. Determine whether to conduct interviews one-on-one or with one interviewer and one note-taker for each interviewee. Do not involve more than two project team members in any interview in order to gain the most honest feedback.

Assess Needs   **27**

PLAN

4. Write a brief introduction to use with participants.

5. Conduct interviews.

6. Determine how results will be communicated, i.e. a written summary report or a meeting with all interviewees.

7. Use results to build appropriate leadership action plans and incorporate actions into the overall Change Management Workplan.

★ SUCCESSFUL OUTCOMES

- When leaders are responding to questions with similar answers

- When the tool provides clarity to the project team about the levels of leadership alignment for the change

- When the participants agree on the actions that leverage leadership alignment strengths and fill leadership alignment gaps

---

✐ TIPS & LESSONS LEARNED

- If other assessments are being conducted, consider consolidating the data-gathering process so people are only interviewed or surveyed once.

- Use information with discretion and share responses appropriately within the organization.

Assess Needs

PLAN

- Consider interviewing not only the business or group leaders but also their staff to get a view from both perspectives.

WHAT'S NEXT

- The results of the Leadership Alignment Assessment should feed leadership coaching, leadership alignment activities, leadership involvement planning and Change Management planning.

Assess Needs

PLAN

✂ The Tool: Leadership Alignment Assessment

Question	Purpose
What do you think the ultimate contribution of the change will be to the future of the organization?	Measure degree of alignment of leadership team around the organization's vision, the change vision and the true purpose of the change for the whole organization
What do you think is the relative importance of the change initiative to the organization as a whole?	Measure degree of alignment of the leadership team around the role of the change in relation to other initiatives in the company. Provide insight into leaders' opinions of the required level of coordination between initiatives
Have you experienced other periods of significant change in your history with the organization?	Gauge the change leadership experience / skill level of the leadership team? Gain insight into the organization's history with change and methods that have been effective or ineffective
Do you view the impact of the change on the organization as incremental or transformational? (Explain)	Measure the degree of leadership alignment around the impact of the change on the organization. This should also drive the perceived need for change leadership planning
What do you see as the major roadblocks to successful change implementation?	Discuss what actions, issues or processes are critical to a successful implementation. Measure degree of leadership alignment around mechanisms that need to be put in place now to improve the chance of success

30   *Assess Needs*

PLAN

Question	Purpose
What do you think are the best ways to encourage positive reception of the change by key stakeholders inside and outside the organization?	Measure leadership alignment around most effective stakeholder approaches. Develop ideas and potential tools for stakeholder engagement strategy
How do you define success for this project?	Determine if there is a common mindset among leadership of how to define success. This is key because the definition of success will drive leadership actions and behavior
Who do you think is accountable for delivering the change results?	Measure alignment of leadership team around roles and responsibilities. Measure alignment around the question of where ultimate responsibility really lies
What do you think the role of a leader is in making this change a success?	Measure alignment around where authority for decisions will reside and leadership accountability

Assess Needs

PLAN

➤ SWOT Analysis

WHAT

- The SWOT (Strengths, Weaknesses, Opportunities, Threats) Analysis is a matrix used to clarify the strengths, weaknesses, opportunities and threats facing the change initiative.

WHY

- To help focus on strengths, minimize weaknesses, take advantage of available opportunities and steer clear of threats

- To better understand and begin responding to the Implementation Effectiveness and Sustainability portions of the Change Readiness Audit

WHEN

- Conduct the analysis during the Assess Needs Stage.

- Update or reference the analysis throughout the project.

☛ How

1. Write down answers to the following questions in the template provided:

Strengths:
  - What advantages do you have?
  - What do you or your team do well?
  - What relevant resources can you access?
  - What do other people see as your strengths?

Weaknesses:
  - What could you improve?
  - What do you do badly?
  - What should you avoid?

PLAN

Opportunities:
- Where are good opportunities?
- What are the interesting trends you observe?

Threats:
- What obstacles do you face?
- What is your competition doing?
- Are the required specifications for your job, products or services changing?
- Is changing technology threatening your position?
- Could any of your weaknesses seriously threaten your business?

2. Use answers to these questions to focus efforts on areas of greatest opportunity and to put issues and concerns in perspective.

3. Develop action plans to address the results of this analysis and incorporate the actions into the Change Management Workplan.

★ SUCCESSFUL OUTCOMES

- When the tool provides clarity to the team on what elements of the environment will enable the change and what elements will serve as barriers to the change

- When participants agree on Change Management actions that leverage the strengths and opportunities of the change and that deal with or minimize the weaknesses and threats

---

Assess Needs

PLAN

✐ TIPS & LESSONS LEARNED

- Consider environmental conditions that are internal to the change, such as project strengths or weaknesses, as well as environmental factors that are external to the change, such as project opportunities and threats.

- Try to gather this information with others if possible rather than individually.

- Consider this analysis from your own point of view and from key stakeholders' points of view.

- It may be helpful to find opportunities by assessing strengths and asking whether they provide opportunities. Similarly, it may be helpful to find threats by assessing weaknesses and asking whether they lead to threats.

WHAT'S NEXT

- The results of the SWOT Analysis should feed Change Management planning and help develop messages for the One-Minute Exchange, Frequently Asked Questions (FAQ) Sheet, Road Shows and other communication.

PLAN

✄ The Tool: SWOT Analysis

Sample SWOT Analysis

Strengths	Weaknesses
Opportunities	**Threats**

Example: Completed SWOT Analysis

Strengths	Weaknesses
• Strong leadership support for the change • Adequate resources on the team • Strong change imperative	• "Flavor of the month" attitude toward change within the organization • Performance measures that reinforce the old way
Opportunities	**Threats**
• New processes can be leveraged across the organization after the project is complete • The change is consistent with the mandates that the parent company are about to announce	• There is limited funding for the project and budget could be cut next year • The manufacturer of the software we are implementing just got acquired

Assess Needs

35

36

PLAN

Plan: Develop Plan

After assessing the needs of individuals and the organization, customized plans must be created. The data gathered from the Assess Needs Stage drives the priorities and actions in these plans. Tools used to plan the Change Management work include:

- Change Management Workplan
- HR Infrastructure Checklist
- Communication Plan
- Key Message Worksheet
- Leadership Involvement Plan

The Change Management 101 Model™

PLAN

➤ *Change Management Workplan*

WHAT

• The Change Management Workplan is a tool for listing Change Management activities, estimating effort required, assigning responsibility and tracking progress.

WHY

• To manage all major Change Management activities

• To communicate resource needs, milestones and timelines to leadership and other stakeholders

• To help hold others accountable for their role in managing the change

WHEN

• Create a detailed Change Management Workplan after the Assess Needs Stage.

• Use throughout the project to guide daily activities, and update it weekly or monthly.

☛ HOW

1. Use the steps in the template provided as a baseline for starting the detailed plan.

2. Add steps to the work plan for the "how" section of each tool as appropriate.

3. Add activities that are needed based on the outcomes of tools as they are used, or that arise without the use of a tool.

4. Identify major milestones (go live dates, design sign off's, merger finalization, etc…) and add them to the workplan. Make sure that the Change Management

Develop Plan

PLAN

work required to meet any given milestone is timed to meet the timeline.

5. Meet with team members to share the plan and agree on a process for tracking progress and updating the plan.

6. Meet with the team on a regular basis to review progress and add actions or make appropriate changes.

★ SUCCESSFUL OUTCOMES
- The plan communicates steady progress
- The team refers to it regularly for focus and priorities

✐ TIPS & LESSONS LEARNED

- Ensure that the plan format is consistent with the project or organization's formats.

- Represent the work in the plan at the same level of detail. A good rule of thumb is to list tasks that require between 20 and 40 hours of work effort to complete.

- The Change Management Workplan and project plan must be tightly linked for the project to succeed.

- Estimate the resource needs and timing based on the expected impacts from the project. For example, if just one process is being changed, the communication work will take less coordination, stakeholder involvement and time than if 15 processes are being changed.

WHAT'S NEXT?

- The Change Management Workplan should be updated and expanded as more Change Management activities are planned.

Develop Plan

PLAN

✂ The Tool: Change Management Workplan

Task Name & Steps	Start	Finish	Est. Hours	Project Member(s)	% Done	Concerns / Issues
Assess Change Readiness (use Change Readiness Audit Tool)						
Conduct quick hit activities based on the Change Readiness Audit to improve change readiness						
Define the areas of most importance for the change based on the Change Readiness Audit results						
Determine which tools will be most appropriate for this project as we know it today						
Communicate results of the Change Readiness Audit back to the organization						
Analyze stakeholders (use Stakeholder Analysis Tool)						
Gather additional information about stakeholders if necessary						
Confirm stakeholder analysis results if necessary						

40   *Develop Plan*

PLAN

Task Name & Steps	Start	Finish	Est. Hours	Project Member(s)	% Done	Concerns / Issues
Assess Commitment levels of key stakeholders if necessary (use the Commitment Assessment Tool)						
Conduct quick hit activities based on the Commitment Assessment to improve commitment						
Assess leadership alignment if necessary (use the Leadership Alignment Assessment Tool)						
Conduct quick hit activities based on the Leadership Alignment Assessment to improve leadership alignment						
Assess the strengths, weaknesses, opportunities and threats for the change if necessary (use SWOT Analysis Tool)						
Conduct quick hit activities based on the SWOT Analysis						
Based on the assessment of needs, define activities and tools that are appropriate to follow. Add action items that result from using tools or that arise based on a need that is identified without using a tool.						

Develop Plan

41

PLAN

➤ *HR Infrastructure Checklist*

WHAT

• The HR Infrastructure Checklist is a list of Human Resources (HR) issues that must be considered during the project.

WHY

• To identify and address HR infrastructure elements such as roles, staffing, skill levels, rewards and evaluation processes

• To promote cross-functional problem solving between the project team, the organization and HR

WHEN

• Create a checklist at the beginning of Develop Plan Stage.

• Update and reference throughout the project.

☞ HOW

1. Tailor the checklist to ensure the appropriate items for the project are listed.

2. Meet with project team members and review the checklist. As a team, prioritize which HR items will be most critical for project success.

3. Meet with HR and site leadership to review findings from project team meetings. Include project team members as needed.

4. Review the checklist periodically with stakeholders. The review meetings should include a cross-functional group of project members, site manager(s) and HR.

42   *Develop Plan*

PLAN

★ SUCCESSFUL OUTCOMES

- All appropriate boxes on the checklist are checked off by the team, HR and the affected managers

- Site managers and employees contribute suggestions and take ownership of the changes

---

✐ TIPS & LESSONS LEARNED

- Not all job changes will be known at the beginning of the project. Review the checklist periodically to ensure that it includes the latest job change decisions.

- Align HR tasks with project milestones. For example, all training must be completed before employees can use the new computer system.

- Meet with site leadership to promote buy-in and allocate time and resources to assist with the tasks. This is important as ownership shifts from project team to the organization.

WHAT'S NEXT?

- The results from the HR Checklist should be used to customize the following tools: Workforce Transition Plan, Training Needs Assessment, Systems and Structures Action Plan, Rewards and Measures Alignment Template and Roles and Responsibilities Template.

Develop Plan

PLAN

✂ The Tool: HR Infrastructure Checklist

HR Impacts Identified

- ☐ We have identified all positions / people impacted by our project
- ☐ We have identified the type of position that will be impacted – represented / workforce / classified / unclassified
- ☐ We have identified any required changes in skill by position / role associated with our project
- ☐ We have identified any changes to the existing organization and reporting structures (new positions, elimination of positions, etc.)
- ☐ We have identified any changes required to performance evaluation / measurement structures (i.e., goal development processes, risk / reward strategies and metrics / tools)

HR Adjustment / Realignment Activities Completed

- ☐ Skill changes and measures of effectiveness have been incorporated into the job description / job role definition process (i.e., jobs have been redesigned)
- ☐ Organization structure has been adjusted to reflect new reporting relationships, new jobs etc.
- ☐ Appropriate changes have been made to position / organization metrics, evaluation tools and reward strategies
- ☐ Impacted jobs / positions have been recalibrated with market compensation adjustments (if warranted)

PLAN

HR Adjustment / Realignment Activities Completed

- ☐ Appropriate changes to the career / job development paths have been made to reflect job / position changes
- ☐ Training curriculums have been adjusted to reflect new skill requirements and ongoing development needs of people impacted
- ☐ Recruiting processes for positions / roles have been adjusted
- ☐ As-is assessment / to-be analysis performed to determine gap in people / positions for new job / organization structure (organization impact assessment)

Workforce Transition Activities Completed

- ☐ Workforce transition plans by position, department and function have been developed to reflect changes in personnel / positions
- ☐ Transition plans have been jointly developed, circulated and communicated to all appropriate people (workforce, site management, project leadership, etc.)
- ☐ Communication strategies regarding job / HR impacts have been developed and are ready to be implemented

Develop Plan

PLAN

➤ *Communication Plan*

WHAT
- The Communication Plan is a detailed listing of audiences, messages, and specific communication vehicles that are necessary to build individual and organizational commitment to the change.

WHY
- To systematically identify, implement and assess communications

WHEN
- Create a Communication Plan in the Develop Plan Stage.
- Use throughout the project to guide activities and update regularly.

☛ How
1. Use the results of the Stakeholder Analysis to populate the Communication Plan with key stakeholders' names.

2. Find out what communication vehicles already exist. Leverage these established vehicles – newsletters, department meetings, etc. – and include them in the overall plan.

3. Determine the key messages (use the key message worksheet if desired).

4. Use the following questions to help create the Communication Plan:

---

46   *Develop Plan*

PLAN

    a. Which stakeholders would be good communicators because of their influence with leaders, peers or subordinates?

    b. What will give the audience hope, spirit and promise and encourage them to stay involved?

    c. What sacrifice or leap of faith should the audience take after the communication?

    d. What frustrations or difficulties should the audience overcome?

    e. When, where and how should the communication take place (timing, media and technique)?

    f. What materials and staffing (i.e. people to deliver the message) will be needed?

    g. What methods will be used to gather feedback on communication effectiveness and to measure support for the change?

5. For each group or person, list their primary issues or concerns, communication objectives, appropriate messages, vehicles, owners, timing, and materials.

6. Update information regularly and review at progress meetings.

7. Regularly review the Stakeholder Analysis / Commitment Assessment to ensure communication is successfully increasing levels of support and to identify any new stakeholders who need to be added to the Communication Plan.

Develop Plan

PLAN

★ SUCCESSFUL OUTCOMES

- Stakeholders are asking questions and seeking more information

- Resistance is out in the open and being addressed

- Rumors are minimized

- The messages reaching stakeholders are consistent and accurate

- Collective wisdom about the project appears positive

- Feedback is positive

✐ **TIPS & LESSONS LEARNED**

- Balance the effectiveness versus the efficiency of communications. Effective communication takes more time and is usually face-to-face and two-way. Efficient communication is usually one-way and takes little time but is less effective. Use a combination of both methods. The communications objective should drive which vehicle is used.

- When drafting the communications, keep the following key elements of good communicating in mind:

  - Simplicity: eliminate jargon
  - Examples: a verbal picture is worth a thousand words
  - Multiple forums: big and small meetings, memos and newspapers, formal and informal interaction
  - Repetition: ideas sink in deeply only after they have been heard many times

PLAN

- Leadership by example: if leaders behave in a manner that is inconsistent with the vision, their behavior overwhelms other forms of communication
- Explain the seeming inconsistencies: unaddressed inconsistencies undermine the credibility of all communications

- If multiple project teams, locations, functional areas or departments are involved, integrate and coordinate the communications to ensure the impacted stakeholders receive consistent and timely information.

- The plan may start small but will continue to expand throughout the project. At the end, it is a good measure of communication work.

- Sample communication objectives:

- Voice of the customer (VOC): gather VOC from affected audiences to develop and improve project plans
- Awareness: build awareness of project scope, key benefits and timing
- Positive perception: understand why changes are required, what the future will look like, what the plan is and how the department or person will be affected
- Buy-in: gain agreement, support, enthusiasm and momentum for the change by helping affected audiences internalize their role in making the future a reality
- Engagement: involve the impacted audience and other stakeholders in planning and implementation by gathering input, recommendations and decisions through workshops, meetings, etc.

Develop Plan

PLAN

- Sponsorship / Support: gain leader sponsorship and support for project recommendations, requests for dollars and other resources
- Reward / Recognize: promote individual and project team success and celebrate wins
- Two-way / Feedback: gather questions and feedback on project scope, approach, timing and impact

- Communication vehicles
  - All-hands meeting
  - Brown-bag lunch
  - Shift meetings
  - Broadcasts, video conferences or newsletters
  - Interactive video
  - Personal one-on-ones
  - Promotional handouts or demos
  - Local bulletin boards
  - Letters or e-mails
  - Documentation manuals
  - Message on pay stub or paycheck
  - Talking points
  - Video tape
  - Brochures
  - Posters

WHAT'S NEXT?

- After developing the Communication Plan, proceed to the tools in the Launch Communication Stage. These tools are used to execute the Communication Plan.

PLAN

✂ The Tool: Communication Plan

Stakeholder Analysis Data

Name	Issues Concerns	Communication Objectives	Key Messages	Vehicle	Owner	Timing	Materials	Progress/ Notes

Develop Plan

PLAN

Sample Communication Plan

Name	Issues Concerns	Communication Objectives	Key Message	Vehicle	Owner	Timing	Materials
Staff	Layoffs	Awareness & Positive Perception	• No layoffs • Overview of plan	• Dept. meeting	Project leader	9/30	• Powerpoint presentation • Feedback form
Nurses	Shift changes, co-worker changes	Awareness & Positive Perception	• Department staff will stay together • Shift schedules will be similar	• Nurse newsletter • Dept. meetings	Newsletter editor, Dept. head	Oct. newsletter, Oct. dept. meetings	• Project data to editor • Key messages to all department heads • Nursing handout
Doctors	How can I ask questions?	Feedback	• Q&A Sessions Schedule	• Hotline & e-mail	Project staff	During project	• Phone number and email needed

Develop Plan

PLAN

➤ *Key Messages Worksheet*

WHAT

• The Key Messages Worksheet is a template that helps determine the critical messages to be communicated.

WHY

• To articulate why the project is important

• To create consistent, relevant and motivating key messages

WHEN

• Use the Key Messages Worksheet in the Develop Plan Stage as part of communication planning activities.

☞ How

1. Review the Key Messages Worksheet tool to develop an understanding of message "cascading". Each stakeholder group should receive two levels of messages. The first level is the three to five overall messages everyone needs to hear and understand. The second message level is stakeholder driven. These messages need to address the specific issues and concerns expressed from each particular stakeholder group.

2. Develop the first level of messages:

   - Facilitate a discussion with the project team to determine the three to five overall messages.

   - Pose these questions: How does this project link to the department or organization goals and vision?

Develop Plan   53

PLAN

Why should others care if this project succeeds? What is the end result and timing? The answers to these questions should address why the change is important.

- Draft messages that answer these questions and vote on the top three. Which message received the most votes? There should be one overall message and a few supporting messages.

- Seek message approval from a leadership sponsor familiar with the project.

- Use the approved messages in all communication throughout the project.

3. Develop the second level of messages:

- Review the stakeholder concerns collected from the Stakeholder Analysis. What support is needed from this stakeholder group?

- Facilitate a discussion with the team about how to address these concerns and issues. What data can be shared? What is in it for them?

- Draft messages that address concerns.

- Meet with a key influencer for that stakeholder group to review draft messages and make changes as needed.

- Concerns and issues will change over time as old concerns are addressed and new ones surface. This is a measure of successful communication but requires the team to be flexible and address new issues as they arise.

PLAN

★ SUCCESSFUL OUTCOMES
- The messages reaching stakeholders are consistent and accurate

✐ TIPS & LESSONS LEARNED
- When drafting the key messages remember to eliminate jargon and use visual images where possible.

WHAT'S NEXT
- The results of the Key Message Worksheet should feed the messages on the Communication Plan.

Develop Plan

PLAN

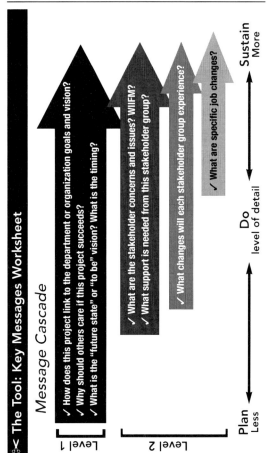

PLAN

Level One Message Creation:

How does this project link to the department or organization goals and vision?

Why should others care if this project succeeds?

What is the "future state" or "to be" vision? What are the next milestones?

Develop Plan

PLAN

Level Two Message Creation:

_____ (name stakeholder group) is concerned about

_____

Write messages that address stakeholder concerns, issues and WIIFM (What's In It For Me?). If some concerns can't be addressed until more project work is done, frame that explanation into a message.

_____

We need _____ (name stakeholder group) to show support by

_____

What will this stakeholder group experience? What specific job changes are known? When will more be known?

_____

PLAN

➤ *Leadership Involvement Plan*

WHAT
- The Leadership Involvement Plan is an action plan for each leader or manager.

WHY
- To clearly communicate each leader's role in the project

- To motivate leaders to be supportive and involved

- To spread ownership and knowledge within the executive ranks

WHEN
- Create the Leadership Involvement Plan at the beginning of the Develop Plan Stage.

- Update and reference throughout the project.

☞ How
1. Work with the project sponsor to determine leadership roles and responsibilities (who is on a steering committee, review committee or communication network).

2. Ask the project sponsor to contact impacted leaders and ask for their commitment to the project.

3. Hold a leadership kick-off event where the project sponsor will discuss the importance of the project and their involvement. Demonstrate tools and distribute information to leadership (action plan, key messages, project data and timelines).

Develop Plan

PLAN

4. Meet with each leader individually.

5. Reiterate key messages and project goals.

6. Ask for their ideas on how they should be involved and offer suggestions.

7. Review and jointly fill out action items.

8. Create an approach for monitoring leadership involvement and progress (monthly meetings, steering committee meetings, leadership alignment workshops, etc.). Each leader should be responsible for tracking and reporting their individual effort.

9. Review the results from leadership involvement plan meetings. Are there concerns and issues? Are there items from the Leadership Alignment Assessment that still need to be addressed?

10. If the areas to address affect more than one or two leaders, consider planning a facilitated leadership meeting to address and resolve issues.

11. If the issues are specific to a particular leader, schedule one-on-one meetings or coaching sessions with that leader.

PLAN

★ SUCCESSFUL OUTCOMES

- Leaders come to the team with ideas, questions and requests

- Leaders are more proactive and less reactive in meeting project milestones

- Leaders actively resolve conflicts and issues together

✐ TIPS & LESSONS LEARNED

- Work with the project sponsor to understand executive conflicts and influence executive involvement.

- Make it easy for them to support the project and offer data and resources whenever possible.

- The level of leadership and the number of executives involved depends on the scope of the project.

- As leaders take ownership of some project tasks, they may have different ideas of how to address resistance and problems. Be open to their suggestions.

- Adapt the level of detail based on what was needed for past leadership involvement.

- Leverage established executive meetings and tracking measures to include the project in discussions.

WHAT'S NEXT?

- Update and expand the Leadership Involvement Plan as more Change Management activities are planned.

Develop Plan

PLAN

The Tool: Leadership Involvement Plan

Directors

The following actions are required from Directors:

Action	Date Required	Date Completed

Managers

The following actions are required from Managers:

Action	Date Required	Date Completed

Participants

The following actions are required from participants:

Action	Date Required	Date Completed

Develop Plan

Sample Leadership Involvement Plan

Directors   The following actions are required from Directors:

Action	Date Required	Date Completed
Conduct staff meeting to communicate key messages and discuss the need for change		
Share impacts of projects with direct reports		
Conduct regular conference calls with staff re: project		
Invite key stakeholders to key reviews, challenge sessions, etc.		
Execute check-ins to ensure team focus and effectiveness		
Invite team leads / SME to speak to your groups		

Do: Launch Communications

After the Plan Phase, the project team or the owners of the change need to reach out to others in the organization. Tools used to launch communication include:

- One-Minute Exchange Form
- Communication Network Table
- Road Shows Agenda
- Feedback Form
- Frequently Asked Questions (FAQ) Sheet

The Change Management 101 Model™

Do

➤ *One-Minute Exchange Form*

WHAT

- The One-Minute Exchange is a speech that communicates the key messages about the project succinctly then asks for support and feedback.

WHY

- To communicate consistent, timely and accurate information

WHEN

- Create the speech at the beginning of the Do Phase.

☛ How

1. Ask each team member to create a draft speech using key messages the team created in the Develop Plan Stage (refer to Key Messages Worksheet).

2. Hold a team meeting to review draft speeches:

   - Ask each team member to write their speech on a flip chart and post it on the wall

   - Give each team member about 60 seconds to read the speech and further articulate any points

3. Suggest improvements if needed and vote on the best speech. If one speech is clearly better than the others, start with that one and make final modifications.

4. Ask each team member to give the final speech to the rest of the group. Provide feedback on the speech (confidence, tone, etc.).

Launch Communications

Do

5. Discuss what to do after giving the speech, and practice asking for input, support or involvement. Gather feedback from the stakeholders if appropriate.

★ Successful Outcomes
• Team members are giving the speech on a daily basis and gathering feedback informally

---

✎ Tips & Lessons Learned
• Use every day as an opportunity to communicate about the project.

• Start a tally board for the team. Ask team members to write down how many One-Minute Exchanges they have each day. At team meetings, talk about the totals and try to break the record the next week.

What's Next?
• After giving several One-Minute Exchanges, the team may want to include information from the exchanges in the FAQ Sheet.

Launch Communications

Do

✂ The Tool: One-Minute Exchange Form

Directions: Review the key messages. In the space below, write a 30 to 60 second informal speech to be delivered at impromptu meetings with stakeholders in the organization. Prepare to give the speech in front of the team.

_____

_____

_____

_____

_____

_____

_____

_____

_____

_____

_____

_____

_____

_____

Do

Sample One-Minute Exchange

- As you know, our current computer systems are slow, unreliable and frustrating. Twenty percent of customers on hold hang up.

- Our response time to customer inquiries will decrease because more information will be easily accessible. Customer service reps will be able to check inventory levels, orders, volume discount schedules and more. Using this new computer program will make their jobs easier.

- Other companies using this software make fewer mistakes, have higher quality and higher customer satisfaction.

- I think the project is right in line with the organization's focus on customers and quality.

- Do you have any questions?

Launch Communications

Do

➤ *Communication Network Table*

WHAT

- The Communications Network Table is a template to help identify and track designated employees in the organization that champion the upcoming changes.

WHY

- To improve the effectiveness of communication by asking individuals from the business to lead and deliver messages

- To improve the frequency and quality of communication by engaging a broader network to assist with communication and feedback

- To reach multiple sites, locations, functional groups or departments

- To involve critical stakeholders in the process (transferring ownership)

WHEN

- Create the Communication Network during the Launch Communication Stage.

- Use throughout the project and update regularly.

☛ How

1. Outline the objectives of the network.

2. Work with project team and site leaders to refine key roles and responsibilities of network members.

3. Identify all stakeholder groups from site, location, functional group or department, etc. (refer to Stakeholder Analysis and / or Communication Plan).

Launch Communications

Do

4. Select leaders and influencers from target stakeholder groups to be in the network and own elements of the Communication Plan. The Communication Network may be at a greater level of detail than the original Stakeholder Analysis.

5. Identify owners at each site to support the network and to ensure that regular meetings occur and that groups know their ongoing roles.

6. Hold welcome sessions to discuss the project and their new role. Share information about the change initiative, including:

   - Roles and responsibilities (see page after tool)
   - Key messages
   - Project timeline and major milestones
   - One-Minute Exchange speech
   - Feedback Form examples
   - FAQ Sheet
   - Key contact information

7. Engage the network through regular meetings, ongoing communications and other forums.

8. Expand the network as stakeholder groups and / or requirements change.

★ SUCCESSFUL OUTCOMES
- The Communication Network is regularly communicating with their stakeholder group(s)

Launch Communications

Do

✐ Tips & Lessons Learned

- Identify the future leaders of your organization. These individuals are not only excited about the change, they are willing to dedicate time to resolving issues and making sure the change is successful.

- Employees are sometimes influenced by a peer more than by a manager.

- Include people who have experienced a similar change initiative to be part of the network.

- Network members represent a change agent body that can be leveraged throughout the project implementation. Be creative about how best to engage them.

- Some employees will fall into more than one grouping. This helps reinforce the messages.

- To decrease paperwork, the network list can be maintained as part of the Communication Plan instead of a separate document.

What's Next?

- The Communication Network owners should use the feedback form periodically with their designated audience(s).

The Tool: Communication Network Table

Stakeholder Group	Communication Network Owner	Additional Influencer (If applicable)

Sample Communication Network Table

Stakeholder Group	Communication Network Owner	Additional Influencer (If applicable)
Surgery Dept Physicians	Bob Jones, MD, Chairman, Dept. of Surgery	Caroline Chambers, Chief Physician
Maintenance Staff	Joe Smith, Manager, Maintenance Department	
Local Media	Carol Lynn, Public Relations Specialist	
Union	Jay Speez, Union Representative	

Launch Communications

Do

Roles and Responsibilities of a Communication Network Owner:

- Allocate time and resources for the change initiative

- Review and learn about the project

- Identify opportunities to reach your stakeholder group. What vehicles already exist or what new ones need to be created?

    - Department meetings, newsletters, Question Box

    - Do you need to seek permission to use any of these vehicles?

- Create a targeted communication plan for your group

- Ask for assistance with certain communication vehicles (as needed). Leaders, project members and managers can make guest appearances

- Enlist administrative support when necessary

- Where offices are geographically remote, identify a backup communicator

- Collect feedback from stakeholder group (see feedback tool)

- Assist with periodic data gathering about project communication within the site, location, functional group or department

- Participate in periodic conference calls about communication effectiveness and progress

DO

➤ *Road Show Agenda*

WHAT

- The Road Show Agenda is a suggested list of topics to address during presentations delivered in multiple locations to help build commitment to the change.

WHY

- To share general communications and build awareness of the proposed changes.

- To provide a forum for gathering feedback from stakeholders about the project.

WHEN

- Deliver Road Shows in the Launch Communication Stage.

- Use throughout the project as needed.

> ☛ **How**
>
> 1. Identify the objective of the Road Shows.
>
> 2. Determine the target audience(s) and how formal the session(s) needs to be. The formality depends on the size of audience and organization culture:
>
>   a. A formal organization and an expected large audience require a more formal or staged presentation (i.e. PowerPoint)
>
>   b. A less formal or smaller organization may only need a conversational style with handouts
>
> 3. Recruit appropriate Communication Network Owners to participate.

Launch Communications

75

Do

4. Schedule the session(s).

5. Develop content and materials to share. The content should follow the message cascade and become more specific as the project progresses. For example, use Road Shows in the Transition Work Stage to share training plans.

6. Advertise the session by using posters, e-mail messages, memos, staff meetings or newsletters.

7. Use a method to obtain feedback (see Feedback section).

★ SUCCESSFUL OUTCOMES
- Good attendance and positive feedback
- Increased buy-in to the change

✐ TIPS & LESSONS LEARNED
- Schedule Road Shows to maximize attendance and coverage. Schedule presentations during all shifts, arrange lunch-break discussions or meet over coffee and donuts.

WHAT'S NEXT?
- Road Shows provide a great opportunity for communication. Use the Feedback Forms and FAQ Sheet with the Road Shows if appropriate.

The Tool: Road Show Agenda

TOPIC	PRESENTER
Introduction	Communication Network Owner or Manager / Leader of Department
Project information	Project Team Member (or most qualified person with greatest understanding of detail)
Answer questions	All presenters take questions
Share communication & participation opportunities	Communication Network Owner
Feedback & close	Communication Network Owner and other presenters as appropriate
Distribute feedback form	Communication Network Owner

Launch Communications

Do

➤ *Feedback Form*

WHAT

• The Feedback Form is a way to collect information from stakeholders.

WHY

• To better understand stakeholder perceptions about the change

• To gather information to help shape future communications

WHEN

• Use the Feedback Form in the Launch Communication Stage.

• Use throughout the project as needed.

☛ How

1. Determine which feedback approaches to use (surveys, focus groups and / or interviews).

2. Review Feedback Form questions.

3. Choose which questions are most appropriate for the audience.

   a. Part A collects qualitative data

   b. Part B collects quantitative data

   c. Add questions from the Commitment Assessment tool if appropriate

4. Before presenting information on the change to a group, tell them that feedback will be collected at the end of the presentation.

DO

5. When reviewing the feedback, look for frequent questions, concerns and rumors. Prioritize what subjects to address and form a response to the high-priority items.

6. Share feedback results with appropriate Communication Network Owners.

★ SUCCESSFUL OUTCOMES

- The majority of the audience is providing feedback

- The project team responds to the feedback

✐ TIPS & LESSONS LEARNED

- The size of the audience will determine how much data to gather:

    – For larger audiences, use shorter and simpler forms

    – For smaller audiences, collect the forms and facilitate a discussion of their responses

WHAT'S NEXT?

- Create a FAQ Sheet to address priority subjects from the feedback.

- Leverage the Communication Network to deliver responses.

Launch Communications

Do

✂ The Tool: Feedback Form

PART A

Please indicate how or if the presentation improved your understanding of Project _____.
We're interested in your opinions and concerns.

1. The benefit(s) of doing the project are

   _____

   _____

2. The challenges of the project will be

   _____

   _____

3. I would like to learn more about

   _____

   _____

4. Managers and leaders seem supportive of the project
   (circle one)   Yes   No

Do

✂ The Tool: Feedback Form

PART B

On a scale of 1 to 5, how informative was this presentation?
1   Very Informative
2
3   Somewhat Informative
4
5   Not Informative

On a scale of 1 to 5, how would you rate your overall understanding of Project _____?
1   Too High Level
2
3   Just Right
4
5   Too Detailed

What project communication have you experienced? (check all that apply)
____ I have read the _____ newsletter
____ I have used the hotline or project e-mail for questions
____ I have attended a presentation or meeting about the project before today
____ I am working with the project team
____ Other (explain)_____

How did you find out about this meeting / road show / presentation?
____ Poster
____ E-mail
____ Word of mouth
____ Manager

Suggestions and Comments

Launch Communications

Do

➤ *Frequently Asked Questions Sheet*

WHAT

- The Frequently Asked Questions (FAQ) Sheet is a reference tool that addresses common questions about the change.

WHY

- To provide consistent and timely responses to frequent questions

- To have a reference sheet for people involved in the communications

- To respond to feedback

WHEN

- Develop in the Launch Communication Stage.

- Use throughout the project as needed.

☛ How

1. Gather all questions and feedback data from various sources. This data may come from Road Shows, One-Minute Exchanges, a project hotline or project e-mail.

2. Review the data.

3. Identify the top priority questions, issues and concerns.

4. Create answers that address questions, issues and concerns and put them in a question-and-answer format.

DO

★ SUCCESSFUL OUTCOMES

- FAQ Sheets are distributed and read

- Fear and uncertainty is reduced because people have answers to important questions about the change

---

✎ TIPS & LESSONS LEARNED

- Make the FAQ sheet one page, eye catching and easy to read.

WHAT'S NEXT

- Share FAQ Sheet with Communication Network.

- Include FAQ Sheet in future Road Shows, newsletters and other communication as appropriate.

Launch Communications

Do

✂ The Tool: FAQ Sheet

Q: Why are we doing the project?
A:

Q: Who is involved?
A:

Q: Can I help with the planning?
A:

Q: Will people lose their jobs?
A:

Q: What is the timing?
A:

Q: How can I get more information?
A:

Q: How will jobs change?
A:

Do

Sample FAQ Sheet

Q: Why are we doing the project?
A: Our computer systems are slow, unreliable and frustrating.

Q: Who is involved?
A: The leadership team, Change Consulting and employee representatives from each department. To find out who is representing your department, contact your department manager.

Q: Can I help with the planning?
A: Contact your department representative to see if there are opportunities to be a tester.

Q: Will people lose their jobs?
A: There are no plans to reduce the workforce. Some jobs are being redesigned to reflect the computers and software being installed. Employees who have redesigned jobs will receive information on training, new job titles and other details from their department manager.

Q: What is the timing?
A: New computer systems will be phased in from March 15, 2009 to April 15, 2009. Each department will get a detailed scheduled about their specific timing and changes.

Q: How can I get more information?
A: Information can be found on the company intranet. Also, you should plan to attend a road show presentation in November. Details to follow.

Q: How will jobs change?
A: Employees who use the current computer systems will be trained on the new system two weeks before converting. More details will be provided as training approaches.

Launch Communications

Do: Transition Work

Part of managing change is transitioning from old ways to new ways of working. These tools address the needs of individuals and the organization in order to support this transition. Tools that support the transition include:

- Implementation Checklist
- Stakeholder Commitment Meeting Template
- Workforce Transition Plan
- Training Needs Assessment

The Change Management 101 Model™

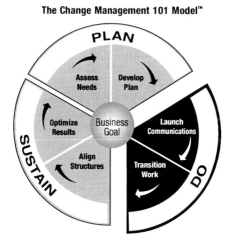

Do

➤ *Implementation Checklist*

WHAT

• The implementation checklist is a list of final preparations needed to implement the change successfully.

WHY

• To manage tactical details that must be completed for employees to be ready for the change

• To categorize activities which must be performed in a logical way so the team can effectively assign tasks to team members

WHEN

• Create and use checklist during the Transition Work Stage.

☛ How

1. Develop a list of everything that is required for people to be ready for the change.

2. Review the list with project team leaders, project sponsors and business owners to ensure that all important areas critical to successful implementation are included.

3. Gather the project team together to review the checklist in detail to ensure that all activities are completed one to two weeks before change implementation.

4. Develop action plans or mitigation strategies to address any items that are incomplete.

Do

★ SUCCESSFUL OUTCOMES
• When all of the items on the checklist are marked as complete

---

✐ TIPS & LESSONS LEARNED
• This list is not exhaustive, and other areas may be critical in some implementations. Adjust the checklist as needed.

• This checklist should be used in combination with the high-level Change Management Workplan to schedule activities and monitor progress throughout the final weeks before change implementation.

WHAT'S NEXT
• If all areas are checked as complete, then proceed with project implementation as planned.

• If all areas are not checked as complete, identify action items to address the gaps in readiness and assign ownership to them.

• Consider consolidating some actions into the Systems and Structures Action Plan if they are related to the organization infrastructure required to support people in the new environment.

Transition Work

Do

✂ The Tool: Implementation Checklist

☐	We have communicated to all stakeholders the reasons and goals for the project.
☐	We have communicated to all impacted stakeholders any individual job impacts and related changes in skills and / or performance expectations.
☐	We have clearly articulated to all employees what is and what is not changing in their areas.
☐	We have communicated what success looks like for the stakeholders (i.e., our expectations of them).
☐	We have communicated the details of implementation / change preparation activities and the support available before, during and after project implementation to directly and indirectly impacted stakeholders.
☐	All impacted stakeholders have attended the recommended training classes.
☐	Where there are competing priorities, we have clarified what stakeholders need to do to support the change objectives.
☐	We have established a functioning feedback process so stakeholder issues / concerns related to the project can be identified and addressed.
☐	We have communicated required changes in goals and performance measures to support attainment of the project benefit goals.
☐	We have created / reinforced key accountabilities for staff to demonstrate leadership support for the project.
☐	Our implementation team is visible and demonstrating appropriated levels of support for the project.

DO

✂ The Tool: Implementation Checklist

☐	Staffing plans have been developed to account for absent employees while at training.
☐	Supervisors of impacted areas understand the increase/decrease in staff necessary to support project implementation (e.g., new system, lower individual productivity).
☐	Cut-over schedule(s) have been communicated to all impacted employees and their supervisors.
☐	A site-wide communication process has been developed to collect and manage issues during project implementation.
☐	Plant/Group Management has reviewed and approved vacation schedules (i.e., critical employees cannot go on vacation during project implementation or during training).

Transition Work

Do

➤ *Stakeholder Commitment Meeting Template*

WHAT
- A Stakeholder Commitment Meeting Template is a planning document for conducting a forum to gain input, agreement and approval.

WHY
- To gather input from stakeholders on the change / design / progress of the project
- To further enroll stakeholders and build accountability
- To align expectations and build common understanding about what is being delivered by a project team
- To build ownership and confidence in the solution or change by leadership, key managers and end users

WHEN
- Conduct the meetings during the Transition Work Stage.

☛ How
1. Determine the appropriate meeting attendees. They should represent a broad group of voices and remain consistent throughout the project. If possible, include people who may be needed for User Acceptance Testing or who are key influencers.

2. Schedule meetings at the end of each phase or at each milestone.

Do

3. Assign project team members to conduct the meetings. They should plan on spending about two days preparing, facilitating and conducting follow-up for a Stakeholder Commitment Meeting.

4. Conduct meetings.

5. Gather feedback and follow up with participants after the meeting to thank them for their participation and share what was done with their input.

★ SUCCESSFUL OUTCOMES

- When the team is gathering useful feedback from attendees

- When attendees express a sense of ownership of the changes

✐ TIPS & LESSONS LEARNED

- Conduct meetings throughout the change as needed, but at a minimum they should be held at the completion of each major milestone.

- Allow ample time to review materials, follow-up and feedback.

- This is not just a steering committee, so include key middle management.

- Insist that directors or key leaders conduct ultimate signoff themselves instead of delegating this role.

Transition Work

Do

- Depending on the specific change to be implemented, consider including the following audiences in the meetings:

    - Directors of affected areas
    - Key managers of affected areas
    - Representatives from all sites / locations
    - Subject matter experts who are part of the extended team
    - Communications Network members
    - Others who are impacted by the change

What's Next

- Use relevant feedback from the group to refine the team's work plan.

- Incorporate any relevant feedback back into the Stakeholder Analysis and Communication Plan.

- Use relevant feedback to design a more effective Stakeholder Commitment Meeting the next time.

Do

♣♥ The Tool: Stakeholder Commitment Meeting Template

SCM Audience	(List names; ensure at least one person is listed from each category)		
Directors			
Managers			
Key Influencers			
Impacted Staff			
Representatives from each location			

Process Steps	How/Notes	Who	When/Deadline
1. Schedule meeting (send invite, reserve location)			
2. Develop detailed objectives and agenda			
3. Designate presenters and facilitators			
4. Develop detailed content to cover			
5. Send out pre-reading material to participants			
6. Conduct meeting			
7. Follow up - confirm outcomes and use of feedback			

Transition Work

Do

➤ *Workforce Transition Plan*

WHAT

- A Workforce Transition Plan is a detailed plan to address changes in roles, responsibilities and organization structure.

WHY

- To identify the individuals impacted by the change and begin to challenge business / HR leaders to determine potential outcomes for these individuals

- To systematically consider how individuals will transition as a result of the change

- To ensure that individuals are transitioned according to organizational values and policies

- To gain efficiencies during the transition process

WHEN

- Develop a plan during the Transition Work Stage.

☞ How

1. Identify an HR contact to help develop and execute the Workforce Transition Plan.

2. Identify specific job titles that require movement of people. Movement can be defined as switching job roles, leaving the organization, changing locations or needing new people.

3. Identify specific individuals involved, naming the incumbents and their supervisors.

96   *Transition Work*

Do

4. Identify the type or nature of movement. Transition types could be:
   - Job elimination
   - Location change
   - Job re-classification (skills and compensation change)
   - New role within the organization
   - New reporting relationship

5. Identify new skills required, such as personal computer skills, project management skills or customer service skills.

6. Determine individual resolution. Sample resolutions could be:
   - Training
   - Relocation
   - Job transfer
   - Early retirement
   - Termination

7. Identify communication needs for people who will be transitioned, as well as for the broader organization.

8. Add comments to help with the communication messages.

★ SUCCESSFUL OUTCOMES
- When all required transitions are carried out smoothly with integrity and honesty

Transition Work

Do

✐ Tips & Lessons Learned

- The workforce transition planning process is a starting place for the project team and leadership to begin thinking about next steps. HR and business leaders must still carry out the transitions.

- HR must be involved in this process and own its outcomes.

- Significant preparation for transitions is required through alignment building across leaders, one-on-one communication and documentation.

- This tool can and should be linked to succession planning and to HR plans.

- The information contained in the Workforce Transition Plan and any related activity is highly confidential. Limit the participants completing this information to those required to be involved.

- Recommend that the project team identify the impacted positions and let the business / HR leaders meet to discuss direct impacts to individuals.

What's Next

- Ensure that HR fully understands the intent of the plans so they can execute the transitions.

- Follow up with HR to ensure that they have executed the transition plans.

- If these activities are part of the Implementation Checklist, go back and check them off of the list to communicate that they have been completed.

Do

✂ The Tool: Workforce Transition Plan

Incumbent and Supervisor	Type or Nature of Transition	New Skills Required	Individual Resolution	Communication Needs	Comments
Names here	Example Transitions: • Job elimination • Location change • Job re-classification (skills and compensation change) • New role within the organization • New reporting relationship for job	List of new skills required for role	Example Resolutions • Training • Early retirement • Relocation • Termination • Job transfer	Define communication needs for the individual/group transitioning, as well as the broader organization about this transition	Thoughts on either the position or the person to be kept in front of the supervisor

Transition Work

99

Do

➤ *Training Needs Assessment*

WHAT

• The Training Needs Assessment is a series of questions designed to determine the type and extent of training required as a result of the change.

WHY

• To provide an overview of the current training infrastructure within the organization, including a summary of existing training and performance support organizations, systems and facilities

• To produce a gap analysis between current workplace skills and those needed to operate in the to-be environment

• To gather information about affected user groups to determine how to best address their training requirements

WHEN

• Conduct the assessment during the Transition Work Stage.

☛ How

1. Review the Training Needs Assessment tool and determine what questions do not apply and what questions should be added or changed to suit the project or organization.

2. Identify the appropriate people to provide information and document those names in the Source column of the tool.

Do

3. Schedule time to interview the sources.

4. Conduct one-on-one or two-on-one interviews (used so one person can ask questions and the other can take notes).

5. Document your findings in the assessment and conduct any necessary follow up to confirm answers.

★ SUCCESSFUL OUTCOMES

- When all of the questions are answered and a robust training strategy and plan can be developed

- When all people impacted by the change are identified and trained on the information they need

---

✐ TIPS & LESSONS LEARNED

- Areas of the Training Needs Assessment may need further investigation as the training development and delivery approaches. This document is just a starting point to understand what it will take to effectively train impacted people.

WHAT'S NEXT

- The results of the Training Needs Assessment should be used to develop a training strategy and detailed training plans.

- If in-house training groups or outside vendors will be used to develop and deliver training, share the assessment with them as a starting point for their work.

Transition Work

Do

✂ The Tool: Training Needs Assessment

Project Scope

Question	Response	Source
What is the overall scope of the implementation?		
Are there any other software or company business drivers that might affect the implementation?		
What level of understanding is there about the changes that will arrive soon?		

End Users

Question	Response	Source
How many end users will require training?		
How many users per department and function?		
List the job titles of the end users and provide a brief description of each title		
How many in each area are heavy users (use significant functionality on a regular basis) and light users (mainly look at reports or use minimal functionality)? Which shifts do they work?		
What are the languages and language skills of the users?		

Do

End Users		
Question	**Response**	**Source**
What is the geographic distribution of the end users? List the location and number of end users by department.		
Are job descriptions for the end users readily available? Where? Do they describe current or future state job roles / responsibilities?		

Training Infrastructure		
Question	**Response**	**Source**
What organization(s) is responsible for employee education and training? What is this organization's role in supporting the implementation?		
What types of employee education and training programs are currently offered (e.g., operations, computer literacy, etc.) and by whom? - Include internal and external programs. Obtain a copy of the curriculum, including a list of trainers, target audiences, locations, and a schedule for each course.		
How is a new hire trained today?		
What type of training is most commonly used? i.e., paper-based, computer-based training, self-paced, and classroom		
What company standards already exist for training materials and on-line systems?		
Have any past training projects been particularly effective/ineffective? Explain why.		

Transition Work

Do

Facilities		
Question	Response	Source
List the training facilities available for end user training.		
Who is responsible for planning and overseeing the details of the training facilities? Training delivery?		
What is the seating capacity at each training facility?		
How many workstations are there at each training facility?		
How far in advance do you need to book your facilities?		
Describe any scheduling limitations that may exist for training?		
Is there a reproduction department or other facility available to support duplication of training materials?		

Do

Resources

Question	Response	Source
Who are the sponsors of the training effort?		
Are there any training resources dedicated to the implementation? If so, how many?		
Who will manage the training program?		
Who will schedule the training?		
Who will customize the training materials and create the exercises?		
What resources are available for materials production (i.e., printing, binding, etc.)?		
When will the training resources join the project team?		
Who are the key subject matter experts? What are their individual areas of expertise?		
What is the availability of the core team to support the trainers?		
Who will review and/or approve the key end user education and training?		
Have you identified trainers? Who are they? What are their areas of expertise?		

Do

Web-based Learning & Performance Support		
Question	Response	Source
If you have an intranet, will it be integrated with the web based learning and performance support?		
What type of connectivity do you have?		
What type of server software do you have?		
What type of web server software is running?		
How much server disk space do you have?		
What type of information needs to get from the web site to the training database?		
Do you have a technical resource that understands and manages hardware, connectivity?		
If you do not have a technical resource, can you outsource this function? Do you have the budget to do this?		
Do you have a web content and migration strategy?		
Do you have someone to update and publish web content?		
Do you have a web-authoring package?		
Do you have people skilled at using your web-authoring package?		
Is there a web graphics artist in house?		
Does your company use a standard browser?		
Have you used web-based training before?		
Is there a standard web based training product that your company uses (CBT Systems, Asymetrix)?		

SUSTAIN

Sustain: Align Structures

Without reinforcing new behaviors, people naturally revert back to old ways of working. Aligning systems and structures to reinforce new behaviors will help sustain gains made through change. Tools used to align structures include:

• Systems and Structures Action Plan
• Rewards and Measures Alignment Template
• Roles and Responsibilities Template
• Knowledge Sharing Agreement

The Change Management 101 Model™

Align Structures

SUSTAIN

➤ Systems and Structures Action Plan

WHAT

• A Systems and Structures Action Plan is a plan for evaluating and addressing changes to the organization's infrastructure so that changes can be sustained. Systems and structures are organizational features such as compensation, rewards / recognition, training, recruiting / staffing, organization structure, and performance objectives.

WHY

• To evaluate HR and other organization systems and structures

• To develop plans to address gaps in HR and other organization systems and structures

WHEN

• Complete the Systems and Structures Action Plan during the Align Structures Stage.

☛ How

1. Review the tool to see if there are other areas that should be added or if there are areas that do not apply to the change.

2. Tailor the action plan as needed.

3. Gather the appropriate people and facilitate a discussion to assess existing systems and structures by using the worksheet and answering questions listed.

---

108   *Align Structures*

SUSTAIN

4. Identify opportunities to modify current systems and structures to build the infrastructure for sustaining the change objectives.

5. Validate this data and information with stakeholders outside of the team.

6. Execute the actions on the plan after validating the data and gaining alignment on the action steps.

★ SUCCESSFUL OUTCOMES
- When all of the questions can be answered and all of the required organizational infrastructure support is identified and planned

---

✎ TIPS & LESSONS LEARNED
- Do not complete this analysis in isolation. Ensure that key stakeholders and HR liaisons are actively involved, and consider inviting representatives from impacted groups.

WHAT'S NEXT?
- This action plan can be used in connection with an Implementation Checklist. Some areas that are 'not ready' in the checklist could require activity on the Systems and Structures Action Plan.

- Update your Communication Plan and Change Management Workplan if needed.

Align Structures **109**

SUSTAIN

The Tool: Systems and Structures Action Plan

System / Structure	What do we do now?	What should be modified or added?	Key activities	Responsible person
Staffing: How do we acquire and place talent?				
Development: How do we build competence and capability?				
Measurements: How do we track performance?				
Rewards: How do we recognize and reward desired behaviors?				
Communication: How do we use information to build and sustain momentum?				
Organization Structure: How are we organized today and how should we be organized in the future?				
Other:				

SUSTAIN

Sample Systems and Structures Action Plan

System / Structure	What do we do now?	What should be modified or added?	Key activities	Responsible person
Staffing: How do we acquire and place talent?	Hire people to be purchasing agents with purchasing experience; strong negotiators	Updated Role descriptions for purchasing agents to be more business partners to suppliers	• Discuss changes to Purchasing Director and HR • Update job descriptions	
Development: How do we build competence and capability?	Basic corporate orientation	Basic consulting skills training; partnering skills and ability to help suppliers resolve their business problems	• Develop training plan • Coordinate with HR • Implement training • Update Performance Measures	
Measurements: How do we track performance?	Contracts managed; dollars saved through negotiations	Conduct 360 feedback; gather input from suppliers on partnering ability	• Develop 360 process • Communicate plan to suppliers and purchasing agents • Gather feedback	

Align Structures

SUSTAIN

Sample Systems and Structures Action Plan

System / Structure	What do we do now?	What should be modified or added?	Key activities	Responsible person
Rewards: How do we recognize and reward desired behaviors?	Basic compensation only (base pay for years of service)	Base compensation plus bonus for business benefit and just in time delivery from suppliers	• Discuss possible changes with HR • Implement changes	
Communication: How do we use information to build and sustain momentum?	None	Newsletter to all purchasing agents and bi-annual conference with purchasing agents and suppliers	• Develop new communication plan • Communicate changes	
Organization Structure: How are we organized today and how should we be organized in the future?	All purchasing agents report to the director of purchasing	Consolidate supplier manager role with external operations roles	• Develop new structure • Present ideas to the Board	

112   *Align Structures*

SUSTAIN

➤ *Rewards and Measures Alignment Template*

WHAT

• The Rewards and Measures Alignment Template is a tool that helps clarify the behaviors that are being rewarded currently and the rewards and measures that will reinforce desired new behaviors.

WHY

• To identify gaps between what is currently being rewarded and measured and what needs to be rewarded and measured in order to encourage stakeholders to behave in a manner that supports the change.

WHEN

• Complete the Rewards and Measures Alignment Template during the Align Structures Stage.

☛ How

1. Complete the template in a facilitated session with the project team. Have the team identify the actions, results and behaviors that are measured and rewarded.

2. Bring in key business leaders and HR representatives to help define new rewards and measures after areas of opportunity have been identified.

Align Structures   **113**

SUSTAIN

3. Ask key questions:

- Does the as-is rewards and recognition program sufficiently support the achievement of both short-term and long-term goals?
- Are the right groups or individuals (key contributors to the success of the change) eligible for rewards? If so, are they rewarded for the right things, are the rewards in line with employee expectations, and are the rewards motivational?
- How well do executives and managers understand and communicate the current reward and recognition plans to employees?
- Who is responsible for determining recognition and rewards (peers, customers, managers, etc.)?
- What should be rewarded in the future to encourage the "right" behaviors?
- Who administers each current plan? How can they be involved in redesigning the plans?

4. Develop a plan for gaining buy-in for the proposed changes to rewards and measures.

5. Assign ownership for implementing the proposed changes to rewards and measures.

6. Validate the data and alignment on the action steps.

SUSTAIN

★ SUCCESSFUL OUTCOMES

- When 'what is important' is the same as 'what gets done'

✎ TIPS & LESSONS LEARNED

- The Rewards and Measures Alignment Template links to the Systems and Structures Action Plan because the organization's rewards and measures is one type of "system".

WHAT'S NEXT?

- After defining the appropriate performance metrics and rewards, work with HR and functional managers to implement them.

- Build metrics into existing performance management processes and forms. Ensure that staff and management understand the changes and why they have been implemented.

Align Structures

SUSTAIN

✂ The Tool: Rewards and Measures Alignment Template

Today – Position X	Tomorrow – Position X
What is important?	What is important?
What is measured?	What is measured?
What gets done?	What gets done?
What gets rewarded?	What gets rewarded?
Who decides what gets measured or rewarded?	Who decides what gets measured or rewarded?

SUSTAIN

Sample Rewards and Measures Alignment Template

Today – Position X	Tomorrow – Position X
What is important? • Negotiating deals • Decreasing costs	**What is important?** • Supplier reliability and quality • Better service from suppliers
What is measured? • Dollars saved • Number of deals made • Number of contracts managed	**What is measured?** • Lean manufacturing at suppliers • Better service from suppliers
What gets done? • Negotiations on price • Bidding process is managed • Adversarial relationship between us and suppliers	**What gets done?** • Better supplier reliability and quality • Better service from suppliers
What gets rewarded? • Negotiations on price • Bidding process is managed • Adversarial relationship between us and suppliers	**What gets rewarded?** • Partnering with suppliers • Reliability and quality from suppliers • Better service from suppliers
Who decides what gets measured or rewarded? • Boss	**Who decides what gets measured or rewarded?** • Boss • Peers • Suppliers

Align Structures

SUSTAIN

➤ *Roles and Responsibilities Template*

WHAT

- The Roles and Responsibilities Template is a tool that clarifies who is accountable for key tasks, who will actually perform the work for those tasks, and who must provide input or receive outputs from key tasks.

WHY

- To define and describe authority over decisions

- To outline who is accountable for the ultimate success of the task, who is responsible for executing the task, and who needs to provide input or receive outputs from the task

- To ensure smooth handoff of responsibilities between the project team and the sustaining business

WHEN

- Complete the Roles and Responsibilities Template during the Align Systems and Structures Stage when the change is transitioned from a project team to the business.

- Consider using the Roles and Responsibilities Template whenever clarification of roles and responsibilities is needed.

☛ How

1. Assemble a group of project team members and business leaders to discuss the ongoing ownership of the changes.

2. Define the activities and decisions required to sustain the changes.

118   *Align Structures*

SUSTAIN

3. Develop a list of all people involved in the sustaining business.

4. Define who will execute, own, supply inputs and consume outputs of each activity and decision.

5. Develop a plan to ensure that all the people listed on the template understand their role and buy into their responsibilities.

6. Assign responsibilities for communicating the plans.

★ SUCCESSFUL OUTCOMES
• When people understand their role and the roles of others

✎ TIPS & LESSONS LEARNED
• This tool can be used for team development to clarify roles and responsibilities.

WHAT'S NEXT?
• Use the outputs of this tool to manage individual activities. If issues arise due to lack of clarity around ownership or accountability, refer back to this document to help define who does what.

• Ensure that others in the organization understand the roles and responsibilities of those with whom they will interact.

Align Structures   **119**

SUSTAIN

✂ The Tool: Roles and Responsibilities Template

Roles and Responsibilities Template						
WHAT: Activities / Decisions		**WHO:** Roles – People / Positions / Groups				

Definitions:

E = Executer — Person or group who actually executes the work or makes the decision

A = Accountable — Person or group responsible for completing the task and delivering the results. This may or may not be the same person as the Executer

S = Suppliers — People who provide inputs into the task or decision

C = Customers — People who use the outputs of the task or the decision

120   *Align Structures*

SUSTAIN

Sample Roles and Responsibilities Template

Roles and Responsibilities Template

Activities / Decisions	Lean MFG Champion: John	Line Supervisor: Mary	Line Associates	Lean Business Sponsor: Jane
Develop lean strategy and monitor progress	E	S, C	C	A
Update visual cues	A	E	S	C
Collect metric data	A	E	S, C	C
Manufacture products	C	A	E	

Definitions:

E = Executer   Person or group who actually executes the work or makes the decision

A = Accountable   Person or group responsible for completing the task and delivering the results. This may or may not be the same person as the Executer

S = Suppliers   People who provide inputs into the task or decision

C = Customers   People who use the outputs of the task or the decision

Align Structures

SUSTAIN

➤ *Knowledge Sharing Agreement*

WHAT

• A Knowledge Sharing Agreement is a contract between two people that outlines information or skills to be transferred from one person to the other. The contract includes timelines for knowledge sharing as well as ways to measure success.

WHY

• To identify key competencies that need to be taught or transferred to another individual or group

• To track progress of the sharing or education process and ensure completion of individual tasks

WHEN

• Complete a Knowledge Sharing Agreement during the Align Structures Stage to build organizational ownership for the project outcomes.

• Consider using a Knowledge Sharing Agreement whenever there is a planned transition of resources.

☛ How

1. Identify information that needs to be shared with or transferred between individuals.

2. Establish deadlines to be met for information and knowledge sharing.

3. Inform the two parties and ask them to jointly develop a Knowledge Sharing Agreement.

Align Structures

SUSTAIN

4. Complete the Knowledge Sharing Agreement:

- Focus on the three areas of knowledge: technical, process and people

- For each skill or area of knowledge, list how the sharing will occur (formal, on-the-job, etc.), action items required to share knowledge, current or baseline skill level, target completion date and measures of success

5. Seek approval for plan with dates and measures of success.

6. Track the agreement monthly or quarterly to ensure that progress is being made toward target dates.

7. Adjust the agreement as necessary over time.

★ SUCCESSFUL OUTCOMES

- When all of the items on the agreement have been successfully completed

- When the base skills are developed within the business to sustain project benefits

---

✐ TIPS & LESSONS LEARNED

- Make actions tangible and measurable.

- Measures of success will be different based on what kind of knowledge is being transferred.

Align Structures

SUSTAIN

- Allow time for people to learn. Do not expect to share all of the knowledge in a single day.

- Approval is important to ensure that key leaders are comfortable with the skills and knowledge levels of managers and staff.

- Use a Knowledge Sharing Agreement whenever there is a planned transition of resources. This could occur when:

  – Someone is leaving a job for a new position and needs to train the replacement

  – Someone is working with a consultant and learning technical skills that will enable them to maintain and update the system in the future

  – Someone is working on temporary assignment with a manager from another department or function and wants to learn more about the new area before the assignment is over

WHAT'S NEXT?

- The results of the Knowledge Sharing Agreement should be monitored on a regular basis to ensure that the knowledge sharing is successful. If the agreement is too aggressive or not aggressive enough, it can be changed.

- If it becomes clear that the strategies outlined or the people chosen to participate in the knowledge sharing are not appropriate, make changes to ensure that the right people are ready to own the changes according to the agreed upon timeframe.

Align Structures

SUSTAIN

✂ The Tool: Knowledge Sharing Agreement

Knowledge Sharing Agreement

Name of Knowledge Recipient

Role of Knowledge Recipient

Name of Person Sharing Knowledge

Role of Person Sharing Knowledge

Knowledge to Share	Method of Transfer - formal training, working session, on-the job, etc	Specific Action Item	Current of Level Proficiency	Level of Proficiency Needed	Target Completion Date	Actual Completion Date
Technical						

Align Structures

SUSTAIN

Knowledge to Share	Method of Transfer - formal training, working session, on-the job, etc	Specific Action Item	Current of Level Proficiency	Level of Proficiency Needed	Target Completion Date	Actual Completion Date
Process/Functional						
People or Interpersonal						

Completion Date: _____

Recipient: _____

Transferor: _____

Proficiency Level
1 = Have an understanding
2 = Ability to complete with assistance
3 = Proficient
4 = Expert/ Trainer

Align Structures

SUSTAIN

Sample Knowledge Sharing Agreement

Terry Nicely	Lean Manufacturing Supervisor
Name of Knowledge Recipient	Role of Knowledge Recipient
John Docier	Lean Manufacturing Consultant
Name of Person Sharing Knowledge	Role of Person Sharing Knowledge

Knowledge to Share	Method of Transfer - formal training, working session, on-the job, etc	Specific Action Item	Current of Level Proficiency	Level of Proficiency Needed	Target Completion Date	Actual Completion Date
Technical						
Understands and demonstrates the skills required to conduct value stream mapping analysis (current state)	Formal training (2 weeks) and on the job training with spreadsheets	Involve in the characterization phase	2	4	3/17/03	
Manipulates and download information from current system	On the job training	Help in information gathering and analysis	2	4	4/14/03	

SUSTAIN

Knowledge to Share	Method of Transfer - formal training, working session, on-the job, etc	Specific Action Item	Current of Level Proficiency	Level of Proficiency Needed	Target Completion Date	Actual Completion Date
Process/Functional						
Understands and demonstrates proficiency of the Lean methodology and approach	On the job training and knowledge transfer (content) available on line	Work every day together.	1	4	5/16/03	
Is capable of providing content inputs/direction to the Lean project	On the job training	Offer input in order to coordinate current analysis and lean deployment on the floor.	1	4	5/30/03	
People						
Can identify cross-initiative dependencies	On the job training	Constant interaction with th Steering Committee for the Lean deployment and current findings from the assessment	1	4	6/30/03	
Identify/Understand skillsets required to implement or support Lean in his location	Workshops	Assign responsibilities to support functions for lean deployment	1	4	6/30/03	

Proficiency Level
1= Have an understanding   3= Proficient
2= Ability to complete with assistance   4= Expert/ Trainer

Completion Date: _____
Recipient: _____
Transferor: _____

Align Structures

SUSTAIN

Sustain: Optimize Results

In order to ensure that the changes yield optimal results over time, new behaviors must be integrated into the new way of working. Tools used to assess how the changes have been integrated and how behaviors have changed include:

- Change Integration Checklist
- HR Measures Form
- HR Measures Questionnaire
- Lessons Learned Process

The Change Management 101 Model™

Optimize Results

SUSTAIN

➤ *Change Integration Checklist*

WHAT

- The Change Integration Checklist is a questionnaire that assesses whether the change has become part of the organization's way of working.

WHY

- To assess whether the changes have been integrated into the organization's way of working

- To understand whether additional reinforcement is needed

WHEN

- Use the Change Integration Checklist two to four months after a change effort is implemented.

☞ How

1. Define the audience for conducting Change Integration Checklist. Survey the entire population if desired, or choose a random sample.

2. Conduct the survey through hard copy, electronic distribution or facilitated focus group meetings.

3. Analyze the results by summarizing the answers and identifying common themes. Pay specific attention to areas where the answers are 'somewhat' or 'no.' These areas may need further assessment or work to develop 'yes' answers.

4. Report findings to sponsors and stakeholders as appropriate.

SUSTAIN

5. Celebrate success if the survey indicates that the changes have been well integrated into the organization.

★ SUCCESSFUL OUTCOMES

- Project leaders understand how changes have been integrated into the way the organization works

- Project sponsors understand whether additional reinforcement is required to make the change part of the way the organization works

---

✐ TIPS & LESSONS LEARNED

- Be honest about areas where the changes are not well integrated. It may be necessary to delve deeper into areas through focus groups or interviews to gain more detailed information about why integration has not occurred.

- Maintain confidentiality or anonymity so participants are more likely to respond candidly.

- Consider coloring the "yes" column green, the "somewhat" column yellow, and the "no" column red to visually reinforce the areas of success and weakness.

WHAT'S NEXT?

- Define new reinforcement strategies (see Align Structures tools) if necessary to integrate the changes into the organizational norms.

Optimize Results

SUSTAIN

✄ The Tool: Change Integration Checklist

QUESTION	YES	SOMEWHAT	NO
Are leaders acting as champions for the future state?			
Are employees excited about the future?			
Is there a safe outlet for feedback – reactions, concerns and comments – for all concerned?			
Are the appropriate tools available to be successful?			
Is there adequate support for people to do their jobs effectively?			
Do people have time to do their jobs effectively?			
Does the organization have the skills / competencies to get the job done?			
Have new training and development systems been implemented?			
Are people well trained to do their jobs?			
Do we build competence and capabilities effectively so that objectives are met and results are achieved?			
Are there comparisons of progress against benchmarks?			
Have new measurement and reward systems been implemented?			

SUSTAIN

QUESTION	YES	SOMEWHAT	NO
Do we track performance that achieves results?			
Do we recognize desired behaviors so that objectives are met and results are achieved?			
Do we acquire and place talent in a way that ensures objectives are met and results are achieved?			
Is the organization structure appropriate for the future state?			
Does our organization structure ensure that objectives are met and that results are achieved?			
Is there a plan for adapting the change over time to shifting circumstances?			

Optimize Results

SUSTAIN

➤ *HR Measures Form*

WHAT

• The HR Measures Form is a tool to calculate key measures such as employee turnover and absenteeism.

WHY

• To determine how measures such as turnover and absenteeism rates have changed since implementing job changes

WHEN

• Perform the calculations in the Sustain Phase after new processes and jobs have been in place for at least six months.

• Repeat annually.

☞ How

1. Determine which group(s) and measures to analyze.

2. Determine the length of time (i.e. six months, 12 months) to assess.

3. Work with key stakeholders, for example, HR, to determine baseline rates for the key measures. These rates should be based on activity before any job changes were made. Other examples of rates to track include quality, process times and customers served.

4. Gather data.

---

136   *Optimize Results*

SUSTAIN

5. Use the HR Measures Form to calculate absenteeism and turnover rates or use a similar form to calculate key measures.

6. Compare these rates to your baseline rates.

7. Determine if there are any major changes in these rates. If you have tracked rate data over several months, graphing the rates may help identify trends or changes.

★ **SUCCESSFUL OUTCOMES**
• A comparison of baseline data to current data

Optimize Results

SUSTAIN

✐ TIPS & LESSONS LEARNED

• Take into consideration seasonal changes that may affect the measurement, especially if the time frame used is less than a year. Stakeholders should be aware of any seasonality that could skew the data.

• Productivity will most likely dip initially as employees get used to new technology and/or processes.

• Turnover can be viewed in different ways (leaving the company or leaving the department). If there are many intra-company transfers, employees may like the company but not their situation in a particular department. In that case, spend time to further investigate the reasons for the transfers.

WHAT'S NEXT?

• Use the HR Measures Questionnaire to better understand the root causes for the differences between baseline rates and current rates.

SUSTAIN

✂ The Tool: HR Measures Form

Name of group or department: _____

Based on (circle one):   6 months   1 year   other (specify) _____

Number of absences [ ]

Total number of employees [ ] ÷ [ ]

Average absenteeism rate per employee =

Number of employees that left [ ]

Total number of employees [ ] ÷ [ ]

Turnover Rate =

Optimize Results

Sustain

Sample HR Measures Form

Name of group or department: _____

Based on (circle one): 6 months 1 year other (specify) _____

Number of absences		25
Total number of employees	÷	100
Average absenteeism rate per employee	=	2.5
Number of employees that left		10
Total number of employees	÷	100
Turnover Rate	=	**10%**

Optimize Results

SUSTAIN

➤ HR Measures Questionnaire

WHAT

• The HR Measures Questionnaire is a tool for gathering information from employees about their experiences with the new technology, new processes and new jobs.

WHY

• To better understand what is helping or hindering the attainment of business objectives and measures

• To identify employee issues that may be decreasing job satisfaction and contributing to higher turnover and absenteeism

• To identify positive consequences from job changes

• To uncover any other negative consequences from job changes

WHEN

• Use the questionnaire in the Sustain Phase after calculating turnover and absenteeism rates.

• Repeat as needed.

> ☛ **How**
> 1. Determine which delivery approach is most appropriate for the situation: interviews, discussion groups or a combination of both.
> 2. Review the questionnaire to determine which questions best apply. Add, remove and change questions as needed.

Optimize Results

SUSTAIN

3. Conduct interviews, facilitated discussions or both.

4. Communicate how the data collected will be used and shared.

5. Synthesize the data collected and group comments.

6. Determine which areas have the potential for the greatest impact and prioritize three areas to address quickly.

7. Identify an owner for each area to be addressed.

★ SUCCESSFUL OUTCOMES

- A better understanding of individual and organizational factors that contribute to the attainment of business objectives and measures

- Input from employees on how to improve the current situation

- Action items that should improve future outcomes

SUSTAIN

✐ TIPS & LESSONS LEARNED

- Sharing the questions with employees beforehand can give them time to think about their answers.

- Provide an opportunity for follow-up either by handing out feedback forms for employees to complete and return or by sending a follow-up voicemail or e-mail.

- Some employees will be uncomfortable being critical in a group setting. Having a third party facilitate a discussion (without the boss in the room) may encourage a more honest discussion.

- Positive comments about the changes can be communicated with the organization as a success story about the changes.

WHAT'S NEXT?

- Repeat this analysis as needed.

- Communicate data gathered and next steps.

- Develop plans to remedy issues.

Optimize Results

SUSTAIN

✂ The Tool: HR Measures Questionnaire

Introduction:

Tell the individual or group that it is common for some things to go wrong when processes and technology are changed. The discussion questions are intended to help supervisors understand what is working well and what isn't. All answers will be combined so no individuals are associated with a particular comment.

Focusing on technology

1. What has changed about your computer system? The software? Information access?
2. What is good about these changes?
3. What is challenging about these changes?
   ↑ *What should be changed to improve technology performance?*

Focusing on process

1. What has changed about your daily tasks?
2. What is good about these changes?
3. What is challenging about it?
   ↑ *What should be changed to improve process performance?*

SUSTAIN

Focusing on the work

1. What is still the same about your job?
2. What has changed about your job that you like?
3. Is your job easier? How?
4. Is it harder? How?
5. What has changed about your job that you don't like?

↑ *What can make your job better?*

Focusing on evaluation

1. How is your performance measured now? Has that changed?
2. Are there new or different pressures on performance? How does that pressure impact your job?

↑ *What should be changed to improve job performance and encourage positive results?*

Optimize Results   **145**

SUSTAIN

➤ *Lessons Learned Process*

WHAT

• The Lessons Learned Process is a process to help the organization gather and share learnings from a change effort.

WHY

• To gain a full understanding of what the organization did well and did not do well

• To provide future projects with information that will help them be more successful

WHEN

• Use the Lessons Learned Process after a change effort is completed or during the course of a long change effort.

☛ How

1. Define the participants. Choose a group of six to twelve people who were involved in or impacted by the change in some way. Make sure the group represents the overall involved and impacted populations in terms of level, function, etc.

2. Assign a facilitator (someone to ask questions and keep the group focused on the questions) and a recorder (someone to take notes and keep the group on time).

3. Prepare for the session(s) by sending an invitation to the session explaining the purpose of the meeting.

---

146 *Optimize Results*

SUSTAIN

4. Conduct the meeting(s) using the Lessons Learned Process tool.

5. Analyze the results by summarizing answers and identifying themes that were shared.

6. Report findings to sponsors and stakeholders (as appropriate).

★ SUCCESSFUL OUTCOMES

- Discussion participants share all relevant information with the group and suggest action-oriented recommendations and solutions

- Future change efforts are more successful

✐ TIPS & LESSONS LEARNED

- People expect suggestions to be followed up, so explain that the purpose here is to develop ideas that will help make the next change initiative more successful. They might not see any short-term changes from what they share. Confirm that the sponsor(s) is prepared to act on at least some of the findings.

- Maintain confidentiality or anonymity so participants are more likely to respond candidly.

WHAT'S NEXT?

- Incorporate learnings from the last change into the next change effort.

Optimize Results

SUSTAIN

✂ The Tool: Lessons Learned Process

1. **Introductions**

2. **Explain the purpose of the session.** Discuss why the participants were selected and the purpose of the session, confirm confidentiality /anonymity, and provide any relevant background on the issue to make sure everyone understands what is being discussed

3. **Establish ground rules for the session.**

   > Be honest
   >
   > Everyone participates
   >
   > Do not criticize other participants' ideas
   >
   > No cell phones
   >
   > Use an issues parking lot for topics that need to be managed off-line
   >
   > Maintain confidentiality

4. **Ask the questions:**

   > What went well with the change?
   >
   > What would you do again?
   >
   > What can be learned from this change that can be applied to other parts of the business?
   >
   > What did not go well?
   >
   > What would you do differently?

5. **Summarize what has been said during the discussion.**

6. **Thank the participants.** Indicate how results will be communicated.

148   *Optimize Results*

About the Authors

Stacy Aaron and Kate Nelson started Change Guides LLC in 2005. Before co-founding Change Guides, they worked for Deloitte Consulting serving clients and helping to shape the firm's Change Leadership practice. They have authored over 100 articles on the topic of organizational change and are often cited as experts in the field of organizational change.

Stacy Aaron is a partner at Change Guides LLC. She has more than 20 years of business and academic experience specializing in change management, marketing and organizational behavior. Stacy has provided change management consulting and training to many healthcare, non-profit, and service organizations. She has taught marketing, management and organizational behavior at Miami University of Ohio and Wilmington College. Stacy earned her BS from Miami University of Ohio and an MBA from the Weatherhead School of Management at Case Western Reserve University and currently lives in Cincinnati, Ohio.

Kate Nelson is a partner at Change Guides LLC. She has over 17 years of business experience working with large and small companies worldwide to help them manage change. Her clients have spanned consumer products, life sciences and manufacturing industries. She earned a BS from the College of William and Mary, an MBA from the Fisher School of Business and an MS from the School of Natural Resources at Ohio State University. She currently lives in Cincinnati Ohio.

Save time and order the companion templates

These templates in Word and Excel are a great companion to your *Change Management Pocket Guide*.

Order and download today!

http://www.changeguidesllc.com/order

Computer Based Training

Best Practices in Driving Organizational Change

2 hours of independent learning about change management

Also available in a bundle including the CBT, Workbook, The Change Management Pocket Guide, The Eight Constants of Change and 27 Electronic Tools and Templates

www.changeguidesllc.com

Connect with us online…go to
www.changeguidesllc.com to learn more
about our latest products and services, read
our blog, and learn more about how to join the
conversation about change management!
Here are some examples of what we are up to…

Download our interactive
Change Readiness Audit App
from the App Store

Available on the App Store

Use it individually or in groups
to assess how ready your organization is
for change and to shape your change
management workplan.

Droid and Blackberry Versions available Fall 2010

 Join the "Change Guides" group on LinkedIn! We want to hear what you have to say.

www.linkedin.com

 Follow Us On Twitter

Ordering Information: 4 Ways to Order

 Call
513-354-9503
8:30am - 5:00 pm EST

 **Web Site**
www.changeguidesllc.com

 Fax
253-369-8884

 **E-Mail**
guides@changeguidesllc.com

Price Per Copy*

1-39	$14.95 per book
40-99	$13.95 per book
100-199	$12.95 per book
200-999	$11.95 per book
1,000-4,999	$10.95 per book
5000-9,999	$9.95 per book
10,000+	$8.95 per book

*prices subject to change

Word and Excel Companion Templates*

Site Licensing Available

* instructions for downloading will be sent upon receipt of order

Payment Methods

We accept checks, money orders, purchase orders and all major credit cards.

Order Form

1. Shipping Address (We cannot ship to a P.O. Box)

Name _____

Title _____

Company _____

Address _____

City _____

State _____ Zip _____ Country _____

Phone _____ Fax _____

E-mail _____

2. Quantity & Price

	QUANTITY	UNIT PRICE	TOTAL PRICE
Book(s)			
Templates			
		Shipping and Handling (call or email for the most up to date shipping pricing)	
		TOTAL	

3. Payment Method

❑ Check enclosed (payable to Change Guides LLC)

❑ AMEX   ❑ VISA   ❑ MASTERCARD

   Card #_____ Exp. date _____

   Signature _____

❑ Purchase order #_____

Bill to _____

Address _____

City _____

State _____ Zip _____ Country _____

4. Request for More Information

❑ Information on products and training

❑ Information on consulting or coaching services

❑ Information on certification

❑ Other _____